Playing
Politics

Playing
Politics

J. Tobin Grant

SOUTHERN ILLINOIS UNIVERSITY, CARBONDALE

 W • W • NORTON & COMPANY • NEW YORK • LONDON

W. W. Norton & Company has been independent since its founding in 1923, when William Warder Norton and Mary D. Herter Norton first published lectures delivered at the People's Institute, the adult education division of New York City's Cooper Union. The Nortons soon expanded their program beyond the Institute, publishing books by celebrated academics from America and abroad. By mid-century, the two major pillars of Norton's publishing program—trade books and college texts—were firmly established. In the 1950s, the Norton family transferred control of the company to its employees, and today—with a staff of four hundred and a comparable number of trade, college, and professional titles published each year— W. W. Norton & Company stands as the largest and oldest publishing house owned wholly by its employees.

Printed in the United States of America.

First Edition.

Composition and Layout by Roberta Flechner Graphics.

ISBN 0-393-92486-6 (pbk.)

W. W. Norton & Company, Inc., 500 Fifth Avenue, New York, NY 10110
www.wwnorton.com

W. W. Norton & Company Ltd., Castle House, 75/76 Wells Street, London W1T 3QT

1 2 3 4 5 6 7 8 9 0

CONTENTS

Preface

Have you ever tried to explain how to play a card game to someone without showing him or her a deck of cards? How about describing something more complicated like baseball or football to someone who has not grown up with the game? Now, imagine what it is like to talk about something much more complex like the legislative process or presidential elections. This is the task facing professors teaching introductory political science and government courses. The most common way that instructors have approached this difficult task is through traditional lectures. If the class is small enough, they might leave time for discussion. Some incorporate videos and documentaries to help bring politics to life. The problem, though, is that like card games and sports, politics is something that makes the most sense if it is actually played, not just talked about. That is why this book exists—to help students better understand politics by giving them the opportunity to *play politics.*

This book presents sixteen political games that are designed to last between 30 and 45 minutes. Obviously, none of these games is going to include every nuance of real-life politics. Instead, they are sketches that show the important features of politics without showing all of the details. In the real Congress, legislators must communicate with their constituents, draft legislation, lobby for passage, work with interest groups, compromise with congressional leaders, and anticipate actions by the president. In the lawmaking game included in this book, the legislative process is simplified to players writing a simple bill that is either approved or rejected. By simplifying lawmaking to a few key elements, players can focus on the importance of partisanship and ideology without concerning themselves with all of the tiny details of lawmaking. The same is true for each of the games. Instead of trying to include all of the details, the games include only those details that are necessary to demonstrate the lesson.

The trick, then, is to design a game that is both not so simple that it does not reflect real-life politics and not so complicated that the essential lesson is lost. Finding this balance has come only after repeated trials and revisions. I began by looking at Michael Laver's *Playing Politics: The Nightmare Continues.* This book presents both simple and complicated games. Along with the games, Laver discusses in detail how the games are connected to real-life politics. But Laver's games are too complicated for most classroom settings. They involve many rules and often include several props or playing cards; some require the use of real money. Most would make for swell parlor games, but I found them too difficult to use in a single undergraduate class period.

I have designed games that give students a chance to better understand politics through active learning. After trying out the games in class, I revised them and tried them again, and then again, and then again. With each new round of trials, I changed the rules to make the games easier to understand. I added details to some games to make them less abstract. I took details away from other games to make them simpler and more to the point. I added new games on other political topics. Colleagues of mine, including Ed Hasecke, Jennifer Jerit, and Scott McClurg, also tried out the games in their classes and gave me feedback on how to improve them. The games have been used in large lectures, small seminars, and medium-sized classes. I have tweaked each game, added discussion sections, and provided materials for instructors. The result is a series of sixteen games that will give students a chance to actively learn about politics.

The foundation for these games is *rational choice theory*. "Rational" does not mean reasonable or wise; it is a word taken from economic theory that simply means that people do what they believe is in their best interest. Rational choice, then, means that people—politicians, voters, and players in political games—will make choices that they think are in their best interests. Economists, political scientists, and other social scientists have an entire field devoted to studying how rational people make choices in group settings. Game theorists study how rational people compete. To see how people should act in political situations, game theorists see how rational people would make choices given their goals, the actions of other players, and the rules of the game. The result has been a richer understanding of how politicians and regular people make political choices.

The games in this book are set up according to game theory models. Each game begins by telling you what your goals are. This is important for two reasons. First, it will tell you what you want. Second, it tells you what other players want. Both are important because politics is about more than doing what you want—it is about doing what you want in a world where there are others who are also rationally seeking what they think is in their best interest. This means that in some games you will need to compromise in order to do well. In others, you may need to temporarily do what is not in your best interest in order to get the best outcome by the end of the game. You may need to be deceptive. You may need to lay your personal political convictions aside for an hour while the game is being played. In short, you will need to learn how to play politics.

The games also have specific rules. Some games have very structured rules that specify who chooses what and the sequence in which they choose. Others have relatively few rules, leaving the choice of how to play the game up to the players. Some games are played by teams; others are played by individuals. How the game turns out depends a great deal on the rules of the game.

As you play the games, you will likely notice that a few things will happen. First, you will begin to think strategically. "Strategically" is another term like "rational" that has a specific meaning that is different from its normal usage. To be strategic is to make choices that may be against your best interest in the short term so that you can get the best result in the long term. In other words, you may choose to lose a battle in order to win the war. When you start to think strategically, you move beyond simply considering what is best for you right now and instead consider the rules and the other players so that you make the choice that will help you win the game. This is an important skill that will not be developed by listening to a lecture; it only comes by actively playing politics.

Second, you will find that some players are adept at making good choices while others are not. Sometimes, players make mistakes. In these games, such mistakes can be very costly. Players may misunderstand the rules. They may think they have a strong coalition with other teams only to find themselves stabbed in the back. Some players may decide to even lose the game so that they can make a statement or to stand on their political convictions. When players depart from what they "should" do, it can disrupt your strategy. But such is politics.

Finally, the games are often unfair. Just like real-life politics, you may not have enough resources to win. Another player may have an advantage. The rules may be written so that you are more likely to lose than other players. Or, you may find that you are the one with the unfair advantage. When the games are unfair, it is not an accident. Some lessons require that players are not equals. Some political parties are more likely to be elected than others. Some countries are more powerful than others. Some states are more populous than others. Some people have voting rights while others do not. The games, like life, are unfair.

Each of the games in this book is designed to help you learn by doing, to take the theoretical and historical lessons from lectures, books, and documentaries and work them out yourself. Instead of learning about coalition building, you will need to form coalitions. Instead of learning about voting, you will vote. Instead of learning about politics, you will play politics. The end result will be a fuller learning experience.

A Tour of *Playing Politics*

There are sixteen games in this book. In this section, I provide a brief tour of the book. For each game I describe the key elements of play and some of the important lessons of the game.

Game 1   State of Nature

The name of this first game comes from a term used to discuss a time when government did not yet exist and people lived "naturally." You will have the opportunity to create a political society. Will you decide to live peacefully or brutally, in harmony or in conflict? Will you create a political society that is fair or one where only the strong survive? This game leads naturally into a discussion of why government exists and what types of government are legitimate.

Game 2   Great Compromise

The Great Compromise was the deal made during the Constitutional Convention. This compromise placed legislative powers in both a House and a Senate. This satisfied both large states, who wanted a Congress in which states were represented based on population size, and small states, who preferred a Congress where each state was equally represented. This game revisits this compromise and shows why states were so adamant about how they were to be represented. You will decide on policy under three types of legislatures—a House, a Senate, and a bicameral Congress. The game demonstrates how changing the structure of the legislature changes public policy, even today.

Game 3 Federalism

Federalism is one of the unique features of American politics, albeit not one that people normally think of as political and divisive. When the states came together to form the new nation, they were willing to give the government more powers but reserved many for themselves. Today, there are still many areas in which states and the national government struggle for control. This game gives you the opportunity to form your own federal system. You will need to use your negotiating skills to forge a coalition that will create a federal system that benefits you. This game illustrates how some federalism issues are settled. It shows how democratic principles, political interests, and compromise shaped the Constitution.

Game 4 Voting Rights

Throughout American history there have been struggles to expand the franchise. In the early years of the union only white, male property owners could vote. Today, there are still some restrictions on suffrage. Each expansion of the franchise was the result of both democratic values and political expediency. This game teaches the importance of the franchise and shows how expansion of the franchise is a strategic decision by political leaders. Should the right to vote always be given to people, or should it be restricted? This game will help you explore this important question.

Game 5 Lawmaking

Each year, Congress considers thousands of bills, holds hours of hearings, and days of debate in order to pass hundreds of laws. In this game the legislative process is simplified to the choice over one bill. It is designed to show the importance of building legislative coalitions and being in the majority. It will help you better understand the lawmaking process in Congress.

Game 6 Veto

A president's greatest legislative power is the veto—he can refuse to sign a piece of legislation into law. This is a very big stick that can sometimes help change public policy. But when is this veto power effective? When is it of little use? In this game, the legislature attempts to pass a bill that states what the minimum wage should be. The president (the instructor) will then decide whether or not to veto the bill. By seeing when the president uses the veto, you will better understand the power and limitation of the president's veto.

Game 7 Budget Cutting

Federal bureaucracies are too complex for Congress to oversee their operations and keep them accountable. The relationship between Congress and the executive agencies is a principle-agent problem. Congress (the principle) must try to get the federal agencies (the agents) to do what it wants, but the agencies have the advantage because it is very costly for Congress to oversee all of their actions. As a result, Congress must use appointment powers, budget cuts, hearings, and other mechanisms to keep agencies in line. This game illustrates how Congress may try to get the federal agencies to implement its policies.

Game 8 Crime and Punishment

One feature of our political system that other countries try to emulate is our independent judiciary because decisions on guilt or innocence, punishment or freedom are determined by the law instead of by partisanship. In most instances, judges are given discretion over how punishment should be meted out. But in some states and the federal government, judges are given mandatory sentencing guidelines. This means that if a person commits a crime and is found guilty, a set punishment must be given. This game illustrates how voting rules can change decisions. It does so in an area that one would hope would be immune to such manipulation—decisions involving a defendant in a criminal trial. The discussion following the game may focus on the politics of the judiciary, the importance of rules, and issues of fairness in the U.S. judicial system.

Game 9 Coalition Building

Building coalitions is one of the most difficult tasks in politics. It takes work to convince people that it is worth joining a cause. Even if people believe in the cause, it often takes more incentives to get people to join a coalition. Political leaders face this problem often. Whether it is getting people to vote, contribute to a campaign, or lobby legislators, it is difficult to get people to not "free ride." Free riding occurs when people are able to receive the benefits of a policy even though they do not pay the costs.

Each team must decide whether or not to join a coalition, and if the team does join one, how much to support the coalition. This game underscores the difficulty of building coalitions when there are incentives to free ride. Discussion following the game can focus on many topics including organizing political movements, grassroots politics, interest group formation, and political campaigns.

Game 10 Campaigns

In the United States there are only two major parties, each of which represents broad coalitions. Why is this? This game demonstrates why in most U.S. elections there are only two major candidates and why these two candidates usually hold similar positions on issues. The game begins with seven parties. With each new poll, the parties must decide whether to continue running for office, change the party platform, or drop out and endorse another party instead. Discussion following the game could include a review of recent electoral campaigns.

Game 11 Proportional Representation

In most U.S. elections the candidate with the most votes wins the office. This is the system that was used in the Campaigns game. In the Proportional Representation game, however, the rules change. Instead of only one winner, each party gets a share of the legislature based on how many votes it receives. This game builds on the lessons of the Campaigns game by showing how campaigns in the United States would be different if the electoral system was a proportional representation system. Discussion following the game can highlight the differences in outcomes and the strengths and weaknesses of each system.

Game 12 Campaign Finance

Most people agree with the old political proverb that "money is the mother's milk of politics." Political scientists are not so sure of this statement when it comes to money influencing legislative votes. This game demonstrates both the importance and the limitations of lobbying and campaign finance contributions in the legislative process. Discussion following the game may focus on lobbying strategies and possible reforms of the political system.

Game 13 Media

Where do you learn about political events? You have a wide variety of information sources including newspapers, magazines, Internet sites, radio, and television. Some sources seek to be objective sources of information. Others are intentionally biased in their selection of events on which to report. In this game, you will be asked to make predictions based on news reports by fictitious newspapers. Each newspaper will predict how much unemployment will change because of changes in the federal budget. Some of the newspapers make good predictions; some are biased. The winner will be the player who is best able to sort through the news and find the "truth." After the game, you will be better able to discuss both how the media covers politics and what role the media *should* have in American politics.

Game 14 Tax and Spend

One of the most basic powers of government is the power to tax. From governments as small as local school boards to those as large as the government in Washington, D.C.—all must decide how to tax and how to spend revenue. In this game, you will sit on a committee that will be deciding a budget. What kind of budget will you create? As you decide on a tax system and budget priorities, you will learn the importance of negotiations and compromise in building political coalitions. Discussion following the game can focus on the variety of public policies that can be chosen by policy leaders.

Game 15 Fairness

Most Americans think that politics should be just or fair. In this game, you will try to come up with the best "fair" budget that you can. This game will follow the same rules as the Tax and Spend game but with an important twist—in the Fairness game, you must come up with a budget before you know which player number you are. As you decide on a policy, you must consider the best budget without knowing if you will benefit from the budget. Discussion following the game can focus on what fairness is and the challenges of creating fair public policies.

Game 16 Foreign Policy

Creating good public policy is always difficult. It is even more difficult in the area of foreign policy because nations must try to change the actions of other sovereign nations. The United States, for example, cannot simply mandate changes in another nation's policies. Instead, the United States must rely on diplomacy, bargaining, and at times military force. While there are international organizations such as the United Nations, the World Health Organization, and the North Atlantic Treaty Organization to help shape policies, there is no world government that can legitimately usurp the powers of sovereign nations. As a result, nations exist in a situation that is much like a state of nature. In this game, we return to the State of Nature game. However, here we add an important feature of the global system—the economic, political, and historical ties between nations. This game can lead to a number of topics for discussion, including diplomacy, bargaining, the use of military force, trade policy, nongovernmental actors, and international law.

Acknowledgments

I would like to thank Ed Hasecke, Jennifer Jerit, and Scott McClurg, who helped me as I experimented with these games. I would also like to thank Angela Pavolish, Katherine McAndrew, Jody Pennington, and Roxanne Weber for their assistance. This book would not have been possible without the support of my wife, Carolyn, and the rest of my family. Finally, I would like to thank Bud Kellstedt and Jan Box-Steffensmeier for modeling what it means to pursue innovations in research and pedagogy.

Playing
Politics

GAME 1 State of Nature

Why is government necessary? Many political philosophers, such as Thomas Hobbes and John Locke, claim that without a strong government there would be those who would steal, kill, enslave, or otherwise oppress those who are weak. To some people, this view is realistic. To others, it is depressing and pessimistic. Why can't people live peacefully and harmoniously without the authority of a government? In this game, teams compete in a "state of nature," that is, a world without government. Your team may decide to live peacefully or brutally, in harmony or in conflict.

GOAL

The goal of each team is to survive and acquire the most property. The winning team will be the one that survives the game with the most property.

RULES

There are two important features to this game.

First, as in life, there is inequality. There are seven teams and each team receives an assigned amount of property (dollars). Some teams will begin with a lot of property, but other teams will have very little.

Team	Property ($)
Team 1	10
Team 2	40
Team 3	70
Team 4	60
Team 5	30
Team 6	50
Team 7	20

The second important feature of the game is that there is no government, authority, or enforcer to ensure that teams fulfill their promises. You must rely on your own power or the support of others to stay alive and prosper. You are free to make agreements with other teams, but you are not bound to keep those agreements or promises. What will you do without a government? One option is to work to increase your property. Another option is to use your power against other players who are weaker than you by stealing from them or eliminating them. Or, you may want to give all of your property to a stronger team in exchange for its protection. The choice is yours.

You are welcome to form a coalition with another team. You may even pay another team in exchange for some protection. However, if another team promises you something and then reneges on the promise, there is no government to punish that team.

"Slavery" in this game means that you have no property and some other team determines your fate. Entering into slavery is a serious decision to make. Once you become enslaved, you cannot take back your property. If the team that you just sold yourself to is eliminated, then you are eliminated. If the team makes a decision you disagree with, you must live with it.

In real life, people can make decisions at any time. However, a game like this could get unruly and out of hand without some sort of order. To help things move smoothly, teams must make decisions one-at-a-time, in order from poorest team to wealthiest team. In Round 1, Team 1 makes the first decision because it is the poorest team, followed by Team 7 and ending with Team 3. The order of decisions in the second and third rounds will also be in order from poorest to wealthiest team.

THE GAME

There are 3 rounds in this game. At the beginning of each round, teams will be asked (in order from poorest to wealthiest team as of the start of the round) what they want to do. Each team has four choices:

1. Invest your property and receive a 10% return.

2. Give some of your property to another team as part of an agreement.

3. Sell yourself into slavery by giving all of your property to another team. This means that you will continue to live as long as they do, but you will have zero property for the rest of the game.

4. Attack a team with less property and take up to $20 from that team. *If the team being attacked is left with no money, then they are eliminated from the game.*

For example, Team 3 starts with $70. It could choose to invest and would then have $77 at the end of the round. If it chooses to attack another team such as

Team 2, then it could take $20 from Team 2 and end the round with $90, leaving Team 2 with only $20. If Team 3 attacked Team 7 instead of Team 2, then Team 7 would have no property left and would be eliminated from the game.

Once a decision is made, the property changes take place immediately. For example, if Team 2 attacks Team 5 in the first round, then Team 2 would immediately increase its property from $40 to $60 and Team 5 would decrease its property from $30 to $10. Team 6 would make the next decision. Because Team 2 would now have $60, Team 6 could no longer attack Team 2; it must attack a team with less than $50. If it decided to attack Team 5, then Team 5 would be eliminated from the game, and Team 6 would receive $10 more in property.

Any team with no property is eliminated!

SCORECARD FOR GAME 1: STATE OF NATURE

To help you keep track of how the game is going, record the decision of each team and how much property each team has at the end of each round.

	Round 1		Round 2		Round 3	
	Decision	Final $	Decision	Final $	Decision	Final $
Team 1						
Team 2						
Team 3						
Team 4						
Team 5						
Team 6						
Team 7						

REFLECTIONS ON GAME 1: STATE OF NATURE

1. What could your team have done to improve how it did in the game?

2. Why did some teams do so well when others did not? Was it their strategies or were the rules "unfair"?

3. This game allowed each team to do whatever it wanted with no control by a government. How would the outcome have been different if teams could only invest and could not steal from one another?

4. Imagine what would have happened if the teams had been allowed to create an eighth team that functioned as a government. This new team would have been given enough property by the other teams so that it could defeat any team that violated an agreement. Would you have supported such a team? Why? If you would not have supported such a team, can you think of other circumstances under which you might have done so?

5. Some people think that Hobbes and Locke were too pessimistic about human nature and that a state of nature would not be so bad, making government unnecessary. What do you think?

GAME 2　Great Compromise

The United States has the oldest national constitution in the world. Yet, in July 1787 when the Constitutional Convention met, the Constitution was not yet created. At issue were philosophical ideas about the role of the federal government and the separation of powers. The conflict was also political. There were many unresolved issues facing the new federal government, and the states sometimes had very different ideas about how to resolve these issues.

The issues facing the states were very complicated, and representatives from a particular state did not always agree with each other. For this game we simplify things. There will be only seven states instead of thirteen, and though we simplify the issues, the lesson will be the same—how does changing the structure of the legislature change public policy?

GOAL

The goal of the game is to pass legislation that most benefits your state. The state with the most points after all three rounds will win.

RULES

In this game each state will represent one of seven states.

	Number of Votes in House: ROUND 1	Number of Votes in Senate: ROUND 2
State 1	5	2
State 2	1	2
State 3	3	2
State 4	6	2
State 5	8	2
State 6	3	2
State 7	4	2

The states will be deciding how to resolve two issues that actually faced the states during the first Congress:

- First, the states had a tremendous amount of outstanding debt from the revolutionary war. Some states wanted the new government to assume the debt. Others, particularly agricultural states, opposed debt assumption and the high taxes that would come with it.

- Second, the new nation needed to decide on levels of tariffs for foreign goods. Tariffs were necessary in order to raise revenue, but states that depended more on exports wanted higher tariffs that would protect them against foreign competition.

Here are the policy preferences of each state:

	Debt	**Tariffs**
State 1	Federal Assumption	Higher Tariffs
State 2	States' Debts	Lower Tariffs
State 3	States' Debts	Lower Tariffs
State 4	Federal Assumption	Higher Tariffs
State 5	Federal Assumption	Lower Tariffs
State 6	States' Debts	Lower Tariffs
State 7	States' Debts	Higher Tariffs

THE GAME

There are three rounds. Each round begins with a five-minute negotiation period where states should discuss strategy with other states. For example, is your state willing to compromise its votes on one issue for the support of another state on future legislation? Is your state willing to form a coalition with another state?

After the negotiation period, the instructor will ask each state to write down its vote for each issue:

- Should the federal government *assume* the states' debts or leave the debts to the individual *states*?

- Should there be *high tariffs* or *low tariffs*?

Once all of the ballots have been submitted, the instructor will read all of the votes. This is *not* a secret ballot. Each state's votes will be made public. After each round, the instructor will announce which policies have passed. At the end of the game, the instructor will announce which state won the game.

A state *cannot* split its votes, just as at the Constitutional Convention the original thirteen states could not split theirs.

How the votes are counted varies by each round:

Round One: House of Representatives

Each state receives a number of votes based on the size of its population. Each state will submit a ballot with its choice of policies. If a policy receives a majority (16 votes), then it passes. Policies that receive *15* votes or less do not pass.

Round Two: Senate

Each state receives two votes. Each state will submit a ballot with its choice of policies. If a policy receives a majority (8 votes), then it passes.

Round Three: Bicameral

In this round, the instructor counts the votes *twice*. First, she will count the votes based on population (as in round one). Second, she will count the votes with each state receiving two (as in round two). If a policy passes both the House (16 votes) and the Senate (8 votes), then it becomes law. But if there is disagreement, then each state receives −1 point because Congress failed to pass any legislation.

At the end of each round, states will be given points based on their success at passing their preferences.

- If your state's preferred policy passes, then you receive 1 point.

- If your state's preferred policy fails, then you receive zero points.

NAME:

SCORECARD FOR GAME 2: GREAT COMPROMISE

Policies for Each Round

	House (Round 1)	Senate (Round 2)	Bicameral (Round 3)
Debt			
Tariffs			

Points per Round

	House (Round 1)	Senate (Round 2)	Bicameral (Round 3)
State 1			
State 2			
State 3			
State 4			
State 5			
State 6			
State 7			

REFLECTIONS ON GAME 2: GREAT COMPROMISE

1. In which round did your state do the best? Why?

2. Does it make a difference for policy decisions to have a separate House and Senate? How does this bicameral legislature affect policy?

3. If you were part of the Constitutional Convention, would you have supported the Great Compromise? Why?

4. What compromises, if any, did you have to make in order to get policies passed that would benefit your state?

Federalism

One of the unique features of American politics is federalism: the national government controls some policies such as trade and foreign policy, but state and local governments control other areas such as education, family law, and election regulations. Federalism is a type of separated powers, but it actually developed in the United States as a result of politics. When the original thirteen states came together to form the new nation, they were willing to give the federal government more powers (more than in the Articles of Confederation) but reserved many for the states.

This game gives you the opportunity to form your own federal system. There are seven teams. Each team represents a state that is currently sovereign over four policy areas: commerce, education, trade, and the military. The seven states have decided they would benefit from pooling their resources, releasing their sovereignty, and forming a federation. What policy areas should they give over to the new federal government? Which policy areas should they retain control over?

GOAL

The goal of this game is to pass legislation that benefits your state the most. The state with the most points at the end of the game wins.

RULES

Each state has decided how much it would benefit from giving power to the federal government for each policy area. Some areas are so costly or ineffective for the state to control that creating a central authority would be very beneficial (2 points). For other policy areas a central authority would also be beneficial, but less so (1 point). For still other areas a central authority would bring no benefit, so the state is indifferent to giving over power (0 points). Finally, some policy areas are very important to a state, and the state would lose out if the federal government took over this policy area (−1 point).

Points Awarded If Federal Government Is Sovereign Over Issue

	Military	Trade	Education	Commerce
Team 1	2	1	0	−1
Team 2	1	2	−1	0
Team 3	2	1	0	−1
Team 4	1	0	2	−1
Team 5	1	2	−1	0
Team 6	2	−1	1	0
Team 7	2	1	−1	0

According to this table, Team 1 (State 1) would most like to see the federal government control the military. If this occurs, Team 1 will receive two points. If the federal government controls trade, then Team 1 will receive only one point. Giving up control on education would neither benefit nor hurt Team 1; it would receive no points. However, if the new federal government controls commerce, then Team 1 will be giving up too much sovereignty and will lose one point.

The game begins with a five-minute negotiation period. During this time, teams should discuss how they will vote and try to discern how other teams will be voting. Four teams must support the federal government taking over the policy area for the new government to do so.

An important feature of the game is that teams will vote on policies in the following order: military, trade, education, commerce.

At the end of the first negotiation period, teams must write down whether or not the federal government should control the *military*. The instructor will read the votes (including the names of the teams) and announce if the federal government will take over control of the *military*.

Next, the teams will vote on the remaining three policy areas. There will then be a short negotiation period (up to two minutes), and then a vote on whether *trade* should be controlled by the federal government. Teams will then turn in their ballots, and the instructor will announce the votes and the decision on *trade*. Following the vote on trade, there will be another short negotiation period and then a vote on *education*. After this decision is made, there will be a final short negotiation period, and then the vote on *commerce*.

At the end of the voting, the instructor will tally up how many votes each team received and announce the winner(s).

SCORECARD FOR GAME 3: FEDERALISM

Record how each team voted and the outcome of the vote.

	Votes			
	Military	Trade	Education	Commerce
Team 1				
Team 2				
Team 3				
Team 4				
Team 5				
Team 6				
Team 7				

Outcome

REFLECTIONS ON GAME 3: FEDERALISM

1. What was the final outcome of the game? Do you think this outcome was inevitable? Why or why not?

2. Based on the results of this game, why do you think we have a federal governmental system?

3. What are some of the areas that you think the federal government should control? What areas should state and local governments control?

4. Were there any decisions that your team made that you wish you could go back and change? If not, were there any decisions that were critical to your team doing well in the game?

GAME 4   Voting Rights

Throughout American history there have been struggles to expand the franchise. In the early years of the country only white, male property owners could vote. The franchise was then expanded to include white males who did not own property. After the Civil War, the restrictions based on race were removed, though the de facto restrictions on minorities remained in place for another century. Women gained the right to vote in the early twentieth century. And finally in the 1970s the age limit was lowered from 21 to 18. Today, there are still some restrictions on suffrage that some people find objectionable. Should former felons or those in prison be denied the right to vote? How long should someone live in a district in order to be considered a resident?

GOAL

The goal of this game is to create a coalition that supports a budget that benefits your team the most. At the end of the game, final points will be given based on how much of the budget your team receives.

RULES

The rules for this game are simple (but your strategy may not be).

Teams 1, 2, 3, and 4 have the right to vote in the upcoming election. Before the election, these four teams will vote to determine whether or not any of the remaining teams should be given the right to vote. Play begins with a five-minute strategy period in which Teams 1, 2, 3, and 4 decide to which teams to give the right to vote, and Teams 5, 6, and 7 lobby for the right to vote.

After the negotiation period, Teams 1, 2, 3, and 4 write down on a piece of paper the names of the teams they believe should be given the right to vote. A team must be approved by at least *one* team in order to gain the right to vote. The instructor will announce which teams have become part of the franchise, but he or she will not say how the teams voted (the teams will have to decide whether or not to trust them).

Next, there will be another five-minute negotiation period. Teams will now form a coalition of voters. This coalition will decide on how to divide the government's budget. The game ends when a majority of the *voting* teams agree on what percentage of the budget to give to each team.

Because some teams are better off than others, final points are awarded based on what percentage of the budget each team receives.

Final Points Awarded, Based on Percentage of Budget

	1 Point	2 Points	3 Points
Team 1	0–19%	20–30%	31–100%
Team 2	0–19%	20–30%	31–100%
Team 3	0–19%	20–30%	31–100%
Team 4	0–19%	20–30%	31–100%
Team 5	0–9%	10–20%	21–100%
Team 6	0–9%	10–20%	21–100%
Team 7	0–9%	10–20%	21–100%

For example, if Team 1 receives 21% of the budget, then it will receive 2 points. But if Team 7 receives 21% of the budget, then it will receive 3 points.

The teams with the most *final points* win.

BALLOTS

Ballot for Round One

Team _____

Should Team 5 be given voting rights?   Yes ( )   No ( )

Should Team 6 be given voting rights?   Yes ( )   No ( )

Should Team 7 be given voting rights?   Yes ( )   No ( )

Ballot for Round Two

Team _____

What percentage of the budget should each team receive?

Team 1

Team 2

Team 3

Team 4

Team 5

Team 6

Team 7

Signatures

SCORECARD FOR GAME 4: VOTING RIGHTS

Record how you think Teams 1–4 voted on the first vote (which teams should vote?) and how much each team received from the budget.

	How Do You Think the Team Voted?	What Percentage of the Budget Did the Team Receive?
Team 1		
Team 2		
Team 3		
Team 4		
Team 5		
Team 6		
Team 7		

REFLECTIONS ON GAME 4: VOTING RIGHTS

1. Which teams were in the winning coalition? How did this coalition form?

2. What would have happened if the first vote on voting rights had produced a different outcome?

3. If groups were given voting rights, was it to help Teams 1–4 win or because Teams 1–4 believed in democratic values? Or was it a mix?

4. How is this game similar to or different from the expansions of the voting franchise in American history?

GAME 5   Lawmaking

A popular proverb among legislators is that laws are like sausage—if you like them, then you should not watch them being made. There is some truth in this. Bills are complicated, and the deals and compromises that must be made might offend our sensibilities. Like it or not, lawmaking is messy and complicated because it requires that (in the case of Congress) several hundred highly opinionated and politically-savvy legislators agree. In this game the legislative process is simplified, but you may still find the process less than pristine. If so, remember that you cannot point the finger at Congress—in this game laws are made by you and your classmates.

GOAL

In this game each player is a legislator deciding how to vote. Your goal is for the legislature to pass a bill that benefits you (and of course your constituents) the most.

RULES

In this game, you will not be playing on teams. Everyone is on their own as a legislator assigned to a political party (Democrat or Republican) and an ideology (Liberal, Moderate, or Conservative).

The game begins with the players selecting party leaders. Players can choose their leader in any way that they want, but it is usually enough to vote by a show of hands. One suggestion: the leader should be someone who fully understands the rules of the game and how it should be played.

Party leaders will take turns introducing legislation to be voted on by the whole legislature. At any time, another player who is not a party leader can also introduce a bill. However, unlike a party leader, a regular player must convince one-fourth of the players to be co-sponsors—i.e., the co-sponsors must initial the bill.

Each bill will include 100 points to be distributed: 50 points must be assigned to parties and 50 points go toward one policy (Liberal, Moderate, or Conservative). Thus, each bill must distribute 100 points in the following way:

50 points must be assigned to one or both of the parties.

Examples:

25 points for Republicans, 25 for Democrats

40 points for Republicans, 10 for Democrats

0 points for Republicans, 50 for Democrats

Each bill will state whether national policy is liberal, moderate, or conservative. How many points a legislator gets depends on the bill and the ideology of the legislator as summarized below.

Points Awarded Based on Policy

	Liberal	Moderate	Conservative
Liberal bill	50	25	0
Moderate bill	25	50	25
Conservative bill	0	25	50

A liberal bill would give liberal players 50 points, moderate players 25 points, and conservative players zero points.

Each bill must state how the party points will be distributed and what type of policy should be enacted. For example, a bill might say "25 points for Democrats, 25 points for Republicans, and a Liberal policy."

The two party leaders each submit a bill. The players then vote for the bill that benefits each of them the most. Each player gets one vote. The bill that receives the most votes wins.

In case of a tie, the instructor casts the deciding vote.

After the first bill passes, play continues with players submitting competing bills. Bills can be submitted by either party leaders or regular players that get one-quarter of the class to initial a bill. The class votes between each bill and the bill that won the last vote.

The game ends when no player is able to submit a bill that can beat the existing one.

Scores are based on the final bill passed—the bill that cannot be defeated.

NAME:

SCORECARD FOR GAME 5: LAWMAKING

Current Bill	Points from Current Bill	New Bill	Points from New Bill	Which Bill Won?

REFLECTIONS ON GAME 5: LAWMAKING

1. What was the final outcome of the game? How was the final bill different from the first bills you voted on?

2. What do you think the outcome would have been if there were no political parties and players voted based only on their assigned ideologies?

3. Is this game an accurate reflection of the U.S. Congress? Why or why not?

GAME 6 Veto

Presidential candidates often talk as if as president they would have control over public policy, promising to make sweeping changes in government programs, taxes, or foreign policy. The truth, however, is that our system of separated powers gives the president few tools to shape public policy. One of those tools is the power to persuade. The president can raise awareness of issues that he feels are important and perhaps rally the public behind him. Another tool is the veto—he can refuse to sign a piece of legislation into law. This is a very big stick that can sometimes help change public policy. But when will this veto power be effective? When will it be of little use?

In this game, the legislature attempts to pass a bill that mandates a new minimum wage. The president (the instructor) will then decide whether or not to veto the bill. *The president will veto any bill that would make him or her worse off.* If the bill is vetoed, then the legislature must pass the bill again, but this time the bill must receive five votes. If the bill does not become law, then the minimum wage remains unchanged.

GOAL

The goal of this game is to create a minimum wage policy that benefits your team the most. Points are awarded to each team based on the outcomes of each round. At the end of the game, final points will be given based on how many points each team received over four rounds. The teams with the *most final points* at the end of the game win.

RULES

Each team represents one of seven legislators deciding on the minimum wage. Each team has a different ideal wage that it would like to see enacted. Points will be given based on how close the final policy is to your team's ideal wage:

Points Received for Each Possible Minimum Wage

	$5.00	$5.50	$6.00	$6.50	$7.00	$7.50	$8.00
Team 1	7	6	5	4	3	2	1
Team 2	6	7	6	5	4	3	2
Team 3	5	6	7	6	5	4	3
Team 4	4	5	6	7	6	5	4
Team 5	3	4	5	6	7	6	5
Team 6	2	3	4	5	6	7	6
Team 7	1	2	3	4	5	6	7
President	2	3	4	5	6	7	6

For example, the president would most like the minimum wage to be $7.50 per hour. If the legislature passes a bill specifying this wage, then the president receives seven points. If minimum wage is set at $6.50 per hour, then the president receives only five points. If minimum wage is set as low as $5.00 per hour, then the president receives only two points.

Each round has a different status quo. This means that failure to pass a bill will result in a different minimum wage each round.

Round 1: $5.50 per hour

Round 2: $6.50 per hour

Round 3: $7.00 per hour

Round 4: $8.00 per hour

Each round follows the sequence of events listed below:

First, each round begins with a different status quo. That is, each round has a current minimum wage. If a new minimum wage bill fails to pass the legislature and the president, then the current minimum wage remains in place for the next round.

Second, the legislature must pass a piece of legislation:

- Each team has the option of proposing a bill. Teams do not have to propose a bill.

- The teams can negotiate with each other.

- For the legislature to approve a new policy, at least four teams must agree on the policy. Those teams will hand the president a bill with the proposed minimum wage and the names of the teams that approved the proposal.

- If the proposal is the current minimum wage, then the round stops and the status quo remains.

Third, the president decides whether or not to veto the bill.

- If the president would receive more points by keeping the current minimum wage, then he will veto the bill. For example, if the new bill is $6.00 and the current minimum wage is $6.50, the president will veto the bill because he would receive more points by keeping the current minimum wage than by accepting a new policy.

- If the president would receive more points from the new bill than from the status quo, the president will sign the bill and it will become law. A new law ends the round.

Finally, if the president vetoes the bill, then the legislature must revote on the bill.

- The legislature votes on whether to pass the bill or to maintain the status quo wage.

- If at least five of the legislators agree to support the bill, then it passes and becomes law.

- If less than five legislators agree on the bill, then the veto is upheld and the status quo remains.

Teams receive different numbers of final points, even if they receive the same number of points during the four rounds. The goal is to get the best possible policy in each round, but some teams will not be successful simply because their views are too extreme for the rest of the legislature. Others will do well because they hold moderate positions. Each team is awarded final points based on how many points it should accumulate during the game because of its ideal minimum wage, the status quo policies, and the president's ideal minimum wage.

Final Points, Based on In-Game Points

	1 Final Point	2 Final Points	3 Final Points
Team 1	0–11	12–13	14–28
Team 2	0–15	16–17	18–28
Team 3	0–19	20–21	22–28
Team 4	0–23	24–25	26–28
Team 5	0–23	24–25	26–28
Team 6	0–21	22–23	24–28
Team 7	0–17	18–19	20–28

For example, if Team 4 received 24 points overall, then it would receive 2 final points for the game. If Team 6 earned 24 points overall, however, it would do better because it would receive 3 final points for the game.

NAME:

SCORECARD FOR GAME 6: VETO

For each round, record the status quo, the bill from the legislature, the president's decision, and the final outcome.

| | Outcomes | | | |
	Round 1	Round 2	Round 3	Round 4
Current Minimum Wage				
Bill from Legislature				
President's Decision				
Final Outcome				

REFLECTIONS ON GAME 6: VETO

1. How do you think the outcome of the game would have changed if the president had no veto power? In other words, what would the outcome have been if the legislature could pass a bill with a simple majority?

2. In which rounds was the president most successful in getting what she wanted? Why?

3. Overall, how important is the veto in shaping legislative outcomes?

GAME 7 Budget Cutting

It's no surprise that Americans dislike the idea of "bureaucracy." However, in their day-to-day lives, citizens rely on bureaucracies for many things. Police departments, fire departments, and the military are bureaucracies, as are our schools, hospitals, and social service agencies. Federal bureaucracies are, in fact, so large that Congress has a difficult time overseeing their operations and keeping them accountable. This difficulty is a principle-agent problem. Congress (the principle) must try to get the federal agencies (the agents) to do what Congress wants, but the agencies have an advantage because of the high cost to Congress to oversee all of the agencies' actions. As a result, Congress must use appointment powers, budget cuts, hearings, and other mechanisms to keep agencies in line.

This game has eight teams. Four of the teams will be congressional committees. The other four teams will be federal agencies. Each federal agency will be paired with one congressional committee.

GOAL

The goal of each group is to make public policy closest to its preferences. There will be two winners—the committee that does best of all four committees and the agency that does best of all four agencies.

RULES

The committee and agency pairs must decide how much money (up to $1 million) to give to one of the agency's programs.

- Each committee wants the program's funding to be limited. Ideally, only $100,000 would be spent on the program.

- Each agency wants a lot of support for the program. Ideally, it would spend $1 million on the program.

Each committee is paired with an agency. For example, Committee 1 is paired with Agency 1.

The game begins with each committee meeting with its agency for 5 minutes. During this time, the two groups may negotiate or develop a strategy for the game. Remember—the committee and agency are not in competition with one another. The committees are in competition with other committees; the agencies are in competition with other agencies.

After the negotiation period, there will be four rounds. These rounds will follow the order below:

First, each agency will write down how much to spend on the program ($100,000 to $1 million). The agency will give this number to the instructor, but the instructor will not read aloud the amount. The instructor will give each committee and agency points based on the following:

- Committees receive points based on how close the spending is to $100,000. Points are awarded based on the following formula:

$$\text{Points} = 100{,}000 - \text{Spending}$$

For example, if the agency gave $500,000 to the program, then the committee receives –400,000 points.

- Agencies receive the difference between the funded amount and $1 million. Points are awarded based on the following formula:

$$\text{Points} = \text{Spending} - \$1 \text{ million}$$

For example, if the agency gave $500,000 to the program, then the agency receives –500,000 points.

The number of points awarded is not announced. Only the agency knows how much it gave the program.

Second, the committees must each decide if they want to hold a hearing to find out how much the agency gave the program. This hearing comes at a cost. To investigate the agency costs the committee (in time and resources) $500,000. The hearing does not cost the agency any points. If the committee holds this hearing, then the instructor reads how much the agency gave. If the committee does not hold a hearing, then they lose no points but do not know how much the agency spent.

Third, the committees end the round by deciding how much to reward or punish the agencies. Committees can give the agencies up to $500,000 more for their budgets in reward for doing what the committee wants, or they can punish the agency by cutting their budgets by up to $500,000. This reward or punishment does not cost the committee any points.

Finally, at the end of the round, the instructor tallies the points. However, the instructor will not announce this total until the end of the game.

There are four rounds.

- The committee with the most points after four rounds is the committee winner.

- The agency with the most points is the agency winner.

NAME:

SCORECARD FOR GAME 7: BUDGET CUTTING

What did the agencies do each round?

	Agency 1	Agency 2	Agency 3	Agency 4
Round 1:				
Round 2:				
Round 3:				
Round 4:				

What did the committees do each round?

	Committee 1	Committee 2	Committee 3	Committee 4
Round 1:				
Round 2:				
Round 3:				
Round 4:				

REFLECTIONS ON GAME 7: BUDGET CUTTING

1. How well did your committee do? How could it have done better? How could it have done worse?

2. How well did your agency do? How could it have done better? How could it have done worse?

3. How important were trust and reputation in this game?

4. How important were the hearings and the committees' punishments and rewards?

GAME 8 Crime and Punishment

One feature of our political system that other countries (including many democracies) try to emulate is our independent judiciary. Having a judicial system that is free from political control means that decisions on guilt or innocence are determined by the law instead of by partisanship. In most instances, judges are given discretion over how punishment should be meted out. However, in some states and in the federal government, judges are given mandatory sentencing guidelines. These guidelines mean that if a person commits a crime and is found guilty, he or she must receive a set punishment.

GOAL

The goal of this game is to persuade the other members of the court to agree with your interpretation of the facts and to hand out a punishment fitting your preferences for how the case should be handled. The winner is the justice who does this the best.

RULES

In this game, each team represents a justice on a state supreme court deciding if a defendant is guilty and whether she should receive the death penalty. Each team is assigned beliefs about guilt or innocence and what type of punishment (if any) should be given. In other words, the team members will *not* be deciding guilt or innocence based on evidence. The evidence and your team's evaluation of evidence remain the same throughout the game. The only thing that will change is the rules for how the decision is determined.

Each team is assigned preferences on how the court should rule in a capitol murder case. You receive points based on the court's decision.

- If the court chooses your first choice, then you receive four points.

- If the court chooses your second choice, then you receive three points.

- If the court chooses your third choice, then you receive two points.

- If the court chooses your fourth choice, then you receive one point.

The team with the most points after three rounds is the winner.

	Team 1	Team 2	Team 3	Team 4	Team 5
1st Choice	Death	Acquittal	Acquittal	Death	Life sentence
2nd Choice	25 years	25 years	Death	Life sentence	25 years
3rd Choice	Life sentence	Life sentence	Life sentence	25 years	Acquittal
4th Choice	Acquittal	Death	25 years	Acquittal	Death

Team 1:   You believe that the person has committed a crime that is worthy of the death penalty. If you cannot persuade the other justices, you would prefer next to find the person guilty of a lesser crime and give the person 25 years rather than send a signal to the public that a first-degree murder conviction does not warrant the death penalty.

Team 2:   You believe the person is innocent and should receive a lenient sentence if found guilty.

Team 3:   You believe the person is innocent, but you think that if the person is found guilty then the sentence should send a signal to the public that if you are guilty of first-degree murder you will receive the death penalty.

Team 4:   You believe the person is guilty and should receive as harsh a punishment as possible.

Team 5:   You believe the person is guilty and should receive as harsh a punishment as possible. However, you believe that the death penalty is cruel and unusual punishment and should never be used.

The court will decide the fate of the defendant using three different types of voting systems.

Round 1: Current System

This system has two votes. First, justices will vote whether or not the person is guilty or innocent of a crime. Second, justices will decide what sentence to impose.

1. Justices vote on guilt or innocence by voice vote.

2. If the accused is found guilty, the justices then discuss among themselves what sentence they should impose (five minutes).

3. Justices decide on the sentence. This sentence must receive the support of a majority of the justices, which will occur when at least three of the five teams hand the instructor a decision with the same sentence.

Round 2: Roman System

According to this old system from the Roman Empire, judges vote sequentially on each punishment. Each justice will vote on the most severe punishment. If a majority fails to choose this punishment, then the teams will vote on the next most severe punishment. This process continues until all of the punishments have been considered. In this game, justices will do the following:

1. Justices hand the instructor a ballot stating whether they vote in favor of or against the defendant receiving the death penalty. If three or more approve, then the defendant receives the death penalty.

2. If the defendant does not receive the death penalty, then the justices will vote on whether to sentence her to life in prison. Justices hand the instructor a ballot stating whether they vote in favor of or against the defendant receiving life in prison. If three or more approve, then the defendant receives life in prison.

3. If the defendant does not receive life in prison, then the justices will vote on whether to give her a 25-year sentence. Justices hand the instructor a ballot stating whether they vote in favor of or against the defendant receiving 25 years. If three or more approve, then the defendant receives a sentence of 25 years in prison.

4. If the defendant does not receive 25 years in prison, then the defendant is released with an acquittal.

Round 3: Mandatory Sentencing

The court must decide if the person is guilty of first-degree murder, guilty of second-degree murder, or innocent of both. If the court finds that the defendant is innocent of all charges, then she will be set free. The legislature has set death as the mandatory sentence for first-degree murder and 25 years in prison for second-degree murder.

1. The justices discuss among themselves what the decision should be (five minutes—first degree, second degree, or acquittal)

2. Justices vote on whether the defendant is guilty of first- or second-degree murder or innocent of both. A majority of the justices must agree, achieved when at least three of the five teams hand the instructor a decision with the same sentence.

NAME:

SCORECARD FOR GAME 8: CRIME AND PUNISHMENT

	Decisions			Points			Total
	Round 1	Round 2	Round 3	Round 1	Round 2	Round 3	
Team 1							
Team 2							
Team 3							
Team 4							
Team 5							

REFLECTIONS ON GAME 8: CRIME AND PUNISHMENT

1. What effect did the Roman system have on the court's decision?

2. What effect did mandatory sentencing have on the court's decision?

3. Under what circumstances, if any, do you think that there should be mandatory sentencing? Why?

4. What does the outcome of this game suggest about how you should interpret court decisions and other political outcomes?

GAME 9 Coalition Building

Building coalitions is one of the most difficult tasks in politics. Even if people believe in a cause or public policy, it often takes more incentives to get them to join a coalition. Political leaders face this problem often. Whether getting people to vote, to contribute to a campaign, or to lobby legislators, it is difficult to convince people not to "free ride." Free riding occurs when people are able to receive the benefits of a policy even though they do not pay the costs.

Each team must decide whether or not to join a coalition and if so, how much to support the coalition. In real life, people and groups can support coalitions in many ways—money, time, labor—but to keep things simple, your team's support will be gauged by how many points you give the coalition.

GOAL

The goal of this game is to build coalitions that benefit your team the most. Points are awarded to each team based on the outcomes of each round. At the end of the game, final points will be given based on how many points each team received over four rounds. The teams with the *most final points* at the end of the game win.

RULES

There are seven teams. Each team has different issues that it would like to see government address:

Issues in Order of Importance

	First	Second	Third	Fourth
Team 1	Civil rights	Taxation	Recreation	Crime
Team 2	Taxation	Education	Housing	Healthcare
Team 3	Healthcare	Environment	Civil rights	Taxation
Team 4	Environment	Healthcare	Civil rights	Recreation
Team 5	Education	Housing	Crime	Civil rights
Team 6	Crime	Housing	Education	Environment
Team 7	Recreation	Crime	Housing	Environment

If a coalition receives 10 points, then it will have enough support and each team will receive points based on how important the issue is to the individual team:

First Choice   5 points

Second Choice   4 points

Third Choice   3 points

Fourth Choice   2 points

For example, if a coalition supporting recreation is created (10 points contributed), then Team 7 would receive 5 points, Team 4 would receive 2 points, and Team 1 would receive 3 points. Each of the other teams would receive zero points because recreation is not one of their top four most important issues.

In each round, each team will decide how many points if any it should give to the coalition. At least 10 points must be collected in order for the coalition to form and for the groups to reap the benefits.

Coalitions will be considered in the following order:

Coalition 1   Environment

Coalition 2   Taxation

Coalition 3   Healthcare

Coalition 4   Housing

Coalition 5   Education

Coalition 6   Crime

Coalition 7   Civil rights

Coalition 8   Recreation

The game will begin with a 10-minute discussion period. During this time, each team must decide how it should support the coalitions (0 to 10 points). *These contributions will not be returned.* For example, if your team decides to contribute 2 points and the coalition does not form (it receives less than 10 points), then you will still be committed to support the coalition's effort; but since the coalition does not have enough support, you will receive no reward.

You may contribute up to 10 points each round, but the most you will receive back is 5 points (if a coalition is created for the issue that is your top priority). It is possible to end up with negative points by the end of the game.

At the end of 15 minutes, teams must write down how much they want to contribute to the first coalition. The instructor announces the result *but the amount that each team contributes remains confidential until the end of the game.*

- If at least 10 points are contributed, then the coalition forms and teams receive subsidies based on the ranking of the item for each team.

- If less than 10 points are contributed, then the coalition does *not* form and no teams receive rewards.

After the first outcome is announced, teams will have only one minute to decide how much to contribute to the next proposed coalition. For each coalition, teams submit secret ballots with their amount of support. The game continues until each proposed coalition has been considered.

At the end of the game—and only at the end of the game—the instructor will reveal how much each team contributed in each round and how many points each team has.

The team with the most points at the end of the game wins.

NAME:

SCORECARD FOR GAME 9: COALITION BUILDING

	Issue	Your Contribution In Points	Outcome	Net Gain or Loss of Points
Coalition 1	Environment			
Coalition 2	Taxation			
Coalition 3	Healthcare			
Coalition 4	Housing			
Coalition 5	Education			
Coalition 6	Crime			
Coalition 7	Civil rights			
Coalition 8	Recreation			

REFLECTIONS ON GAME 9: COALITION BUILDING

1. How would you describe the outcomes of this game? Were they what you expected when you started?

2. What does this game teach you about the difficulty of forming coalitions? What do you think is necessary for a coalition to form?

3. In the United States, people often complain that not enough citizens are involved in politics. How does this game shed light on why some people decide not to become politically involved?

GAME 10   Campaigns

Ever wonder why there are only two major parties in the United States? It is not a legal requirement—the Constitution does not even mention political parties. Yet, throughout American history there have been only two major political parties at one time. Since 1860, the two have been the Republican and the Democratic parties. Occasionally third parties have emerged, but they die off very quickly, and their main causes are usurped by one of the major parties. In other democracies the situation is very different. There are often many parties, most of which represent specific issues or groups. There are parties that promote environmentalism, nationalism, or communism. There are parties representing religious groups, workers, or white supremacists. There are even parties that represent very specific industries, such as the former Beer Party in Poland. In the United States there are only two parties, each of which represents a broad coalition. Why is this?

GOAL

The goal of this game is to win a majority of the vote in an election by choosing the right strategy to get the most votes. Each team represents a political party. Some parties are liberal, some are moderate, and some are conservative. Teams gain votes by either moving their positions or by joining another party in a coalition. Teams that are part of the final winning coalition win the game.

RULES

Each team represents a political party that cares only about winning an election. This means that even though a team starts off liberal or conservative, it can change its policy positions in order to garner more votes. Just as in politics we talk about candidates and parties as being "left" or "right," we can put parties and voters on a left-to-right scale. In this game, the most liberal position is 0. The most conservative position is 100.

   Voters in this election care about only one thing—which party is closer to their ideology. For example, a moderate voter (50) is closer to Team 2 than to any other party so he or she would vote for Team 2.

In each round parties are told what percentage of the public supports them. Parties can then do one of three things:

First, a party may decide to stay put. If the party thinks that its ideological position is a good one, then it may decide to stay put. This could be a sound strategy because only one team can be at an ideological position. For example, if Team 1 is at 10, then no other party can move to 10.

Second, a party may decide to move along the left-to-right scale. However, a party cannot do this freely. Voters may be upset by a party changing its positions. To account for their actions, parties must spend campaign funds if they move. Each 1 point move costs $5,000. For example, if a party moves from 10 to 20, then the team must pay $50,000. *Each team starts with $50,000.*

Third, one party may decide to merge with another party. Parties may join another party at no cost. There are two restrictions, however. First, a party may only merge with another party directly left or right of the party's current position. Second, the party wanting to merge must get the approval of the other party. Once one party merges with another party, the two parties cannot separate. The merging party must abide by the decisions of the new party and share in the new party's success or failure. The merging party's money becomes part of the new party's budget.

Round 1

In Round 1, parties are assigned to the following initial positions on the left-to-right scale:

Team 1	5
Team 2	45
Team 3	75
Team 4	65
Team 5	20
Team 6	25
Team 7	90

The instructor will tell you the results of the first poll. You will not be told how many voters are at each position, but you will be informed how many voters prefer your party to all others. For example, if your team is told that 20% of the public supports you, then 20% of the voters are closer to your position than to any other party's position.

Rounds 2 through 5

Each round begins with a five-minute period of negotiation and strategizing. During this time, each party must decide to do one of the following three things:

1. Remain in the same place.

2. Move to another position (this is costly).

3. Merge with another party.

At the end of the negotiation period, each team must publicly declare its decision for the round. The team with the highest percentage of the vote in the previous poll goes first. The other teams then announce their positions in order of percentage of the vote received in the previous poll.

The winner is the party with the most votes after Round 5.

NAME:

SCORECARD FOR GAME 10: CAMPAIGNS

Round 1: First Poll

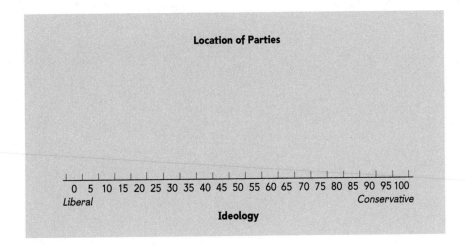

Poll results:

Team 1

Team 2

Team 3

Team 4

Team 5

Team 6

Team 7

SCORECARD FOR GAME 10—CONTINUED

Round 2: Second Poll

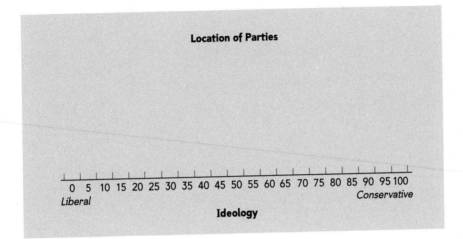

Poll results:

Team 1

Team 2

Team 3

Team 4

Team 5

Team 6

Team 7

SCORECARD FOR GAME 10—CONTINUED

Round 3: Third Poll

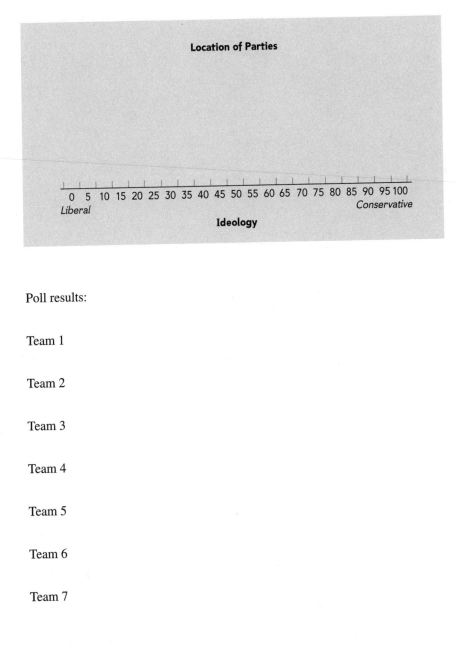

Location of Parties

0 5 10 15 20 25 30 35 40 45 50 55 60 65 70 75 80 85 90 95 100

Liberal   *Conservative*

Ideology

Poll results:

Team 1

Team 2

Team 3

Team 4

Team 5

Team 6

Team 7

SCORECARD FOR GAME 10—CONTINUED

Round 4: Final Poll

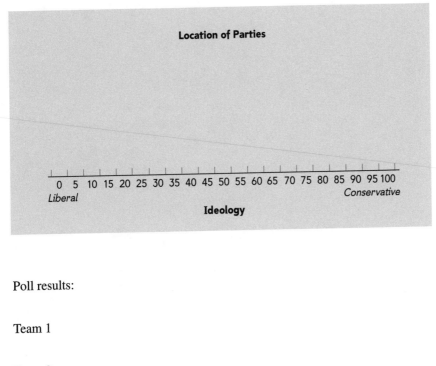

Poll results:

Team 1

Team 2

Team 3

Team 4

Team 5

Team 6

Team 7

SCORECARD FOR GAME 10—CONTINUED

Round 5: Election Day

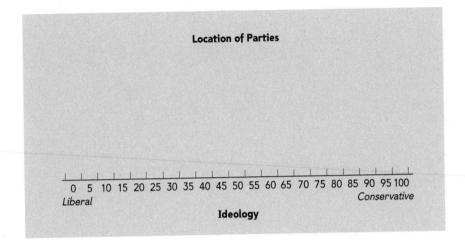

Election results:

Team 1

Team 2

Team 3

Team 4

Team 5

Team 6

Team 7

REFLECTIONS ON GAME 10: CAMPAIGNS

1. How many teams (or coalitions of teams) remained at the end of the game? Which teams were on the winning side?

2. Why do you think there are only two major political parties in the United States? And why are they (relatively speaking) similar with regard to many policies?

3. Do you think that this game accurately reflected political campaigns in the United States? Why or why not?

Proportional Representation

In the United States most elections are decided by a "first-past-the-post" method. This means that the candidate with the most votes wins the office. This is the system that was used in Game 10: Campaigns. In this game, however, the rules change. Instead of only one winner, each party gets a share of the legislature based on how many votes the party receives.

GOAL

The goal of this game is to build a coalition that moves policy close to your team's preferences.

RULES

Each team represents a political party that cares only about winning the most votes possible. Each team can change their policy positions in order to garner more votes. As in the Campaigns game, the most liberal position is 0. The most conservative position is 100.

Voters in this election care about only one thing—which party is closer to their ideology. For example, a moderate voter (50) is closer to Team 2 than to any other party so a moderate voter would vote for Team 2.

In each round parties are told what percentage of the public supports them. Parties can then do one of three things:

First, a party may decide to stay put. If the party thinks that its ideological position is a good one, then it may decide not to move. This could be a sound strategy because only one team can be at an ideological position. For example, if Team 1 is at 10, then no other party can move to 10.

Second, a party may decide to move along the left-to-right scale. However, a party cannot make this decision freely. Voters may be upset by a party changing its positions. To account for their actions, parties must spend campaign funds if they move. Each 1 point move costs $5,000. For example, if a party moves from 10 to 20, then the team must pay $50,000. *Each team starts with $50,000.*

Third, one party may decide to merge with another party. A party may join another party at no cost. The only restriction is that a party may only merge with a party directly left or right of the party's current position. Once one party merges with another, the two cannot separate, and the merging party must abide by the decisions of the new party and share in the new party's success or failure. The merging party's money becomes part of the new party's budget.

There is one campaign round and then one coalition round.

Round 1: Pre-Election Poll

In Round 1, parties are assigned to the following initial positions (these are the same as in the campaign game):

Team 1	5
Team 2	45
Team 3	75
Team 4	65
Team 5	20
Team 6	25
Team 7	90

The instructor will tell you the results of the first poll. You will not be told how many voters are at each position, but you will be informed how many voters would prefer your party to other parties. For example, if your team is told that 20% of the public supports you, then 20% of the voters are closer to your position than to any other party's position.

Round 2: Campaign and Election

This round begins with a five-minute period of negotiation and strategizing. During this time, each party must decide to do one of the following three things:

1. Remain in the same place.

2. Move to another position (this is costly).

3. Merge with another party.

At the end of the negotiation period, each team must publicly declare its decision for the round. The team with the highest percentage of the vote in the previous poll goes first. The other teams then announce their positions in order of percentage of the vote in the pre-election poll.

At the end of the round, the instructor will announce how many members of the legislature each team received. Parties receive one member for each percentage of the vote they received.

Round 3: Forming a Coalition

In this round, teams must try to form a majority coalition that can agree on where policy should be. For example, a coalition may decide to place policy at "40." This coalition must include enough teams so that at least 51 legislators are part of the coalition.

Final Score

Teams receive points based on how close the final policy is to their final position. The teams that are closest (and therefore have the least points) win.

For example, if the coalition in Round 3 set policy at 40, then teams receive the following points if they were at one of the final positions below:

Final Positions	Final Points if Policy Is at 40
10	30
45	5
70	30
65	25

NAME:

SCORECARD FOR GAME 11: PROPORTIONAL REPRESENTATION

Round 1: First Poll

Poll results:

	Position	Percentage of the Poll
Team 1		
Team 2		
Team 3		
Team 4		
Team 5		
Team 6		
Team 7		

Round 2: Campaign and Election

Election results:

	Position	Number of Legislators
Team 1		
Team 2		
Team 3		
Team 4		
Team 5		
Team 6		
Team 7		

Round 3: Forming a Coalition

Who is in the majority coalition? What is the final policy?

REFLECTIONS ON GAME 11: PROPORTIONAL REPRESENTATION

1. How did the outcome of this game differ from the outcome of the campaigns game?

2. How does campaigning in a proportional representation system differ from campaigning in the U.S. system of first-past-the-post?

3. Which do you think is better—the U.S. system or a proportional representation system? Why?

GAME 12   Campaign Finance

In 2002, Congress passed the first major reforms to the campaign finance system in over 20 years. These reforms are intended to close some of the loopholes in the current system. Immediately after the reforms were signed into law, interest groups filed suit claiming that some of the reforms are unconstitutional. Some politicians criticized the reforms because they leave some loopholes open; other politicians criticized the reforms because they go too far. Whether or not the reforms "work" remains to be seen. It is also unclear if the reforms will change the public's perception that groups with money can "buy" votes in Congress.

Does money buy votes? If so, whose votes does it buy? In this game you will try to answer these questions.

GOAL

Each person is independent. Each player is a political action committee (PAC) or a legislator and can decide how to vote. The goal of the game is to have the legislature pass a bill that benefits you (and of course your constituents) the most.

RULES

Each player is assigned a role: PAC or legislator.

Each player is also assigned an ideological group: very liberal, liberal, moderate, conservative, or very conservative.

There will be two winners in this game, the PAC with the most points at the end of the game, and the legislator with the most points at the end of the game.

At the start of the game, each PAC gets 10 markers. The markers may be paper clips, poker chips, pieces of paper, fake money, straws, or whatever else the instructor wants to use. Each marker represents one point. Legislators receive no points.

The game begins with a 20-minute lobbying period. During this time, PACs can bribe legislators by giving them points in exchange for their votes on a tax-cut bill. PACs can give as many points as they want to whichever legislators they want. Legislators can promise anything, but they do not need to keep their promises—PACs must decide whether to trust them.

At the end of the lobbying period, each legislator will write down whether she is voting for or against the tax-cut bill. These votes will be handed to the instructor, who will read the votes and announce whether or not the bill passes. The bill needs a majority of the legislators' votes in order to pass.

Players receive points based on the legislators' decision.

	Points player receives if the bill passes	Points player receives if the bill does not pass
Very liberal	0 points	20 points
Liberal	5 points	15 points
Moderate	10 points	10 points
Conservative	15 points	5 points
Very conservative	20 points	0 points

For example, if the bill passes liberal legislators and PACs receive 5 points. If the bill does not pass, liberals receive 15 points.

PACs add these points to the points they kept and did not give to legislators during lobbying. The PAC winner is the PAC with the most points.

Legislators add these points to the points they received from PACs during lobbying. The legislator winner is the legislator with the most points.

NAME:

SCORECARD FOR GAME 12: CAMPAIGN FINANCE

If you're a PAC: Whom did you give points to? How did they vote?

If you're a legislator: Who gave you points? How did you vote?

In general, how did the following groups vote:

Very liberal legislators

Liberal legislators

Moderate legislators

Conservative legislators

Very conservative legislators

REFLECTIONS ON GAME 12: CAMPAIGN FINANCE

1. What type of PAC did the best in this game? What ideology did the PAC have? What was its strategy?

2. What type of legislator did the best in this game? What ideology did she have? What was her strategy?

3. Do you think that votes can be bought? In other words, do you think legislators change their votes based on PAC campaign contributions?

GAME 13   Media

The media has changed a great deal since Benjamin Franklin was publishing his newspapers. Today citizens have a wide variety of information sources including newspapers, magazines, internet sites, radio, and television. Some sources seek to be objective sources of information. Others are intentionally biased in their selection of events on which to report. Few if any portray the news with complete accuracy. How should you sort through all of the different sources and slants on the news?

In this game, you will be asked to make predictions based on news reports by some fictitious newspapers: *Times*, *Chronicle*, *Post*, *Record*, and *Dispatch*. Each newspaper will make a prediction about future events. Specifically, the newspapers will predict how much unemployment will change because of changes in the federal budget. Some of the newspapers will make good predictions; some will be biased. The winner will be the player who is best able to sort through the news and find the "truth."

GOAL

The goal of this game is to make accurate predictions based on your interpretation of the news and your discussions with other players. The winner will be the student with the *fewest* points after five rounds.

RULES

There are six rounds, but the first round is a practice round. Rounds 2 through 6 will be used to decide the winner of the game. Each round follows a simple order of play.

1. The instructor will post headlines from the five newspapers. Each newspaper will predict how much unemployment will increase or decrease because of changes in the budget. For example, the headlines might read:

   Times: "Unemployment Will Jump by Three"

   Chronicle: "Jobless Rate to Increase by One"

Post: "Unemployment to Remain Steady—No Change"

Record: "Joblessness Likely to Decrease by Two Points"

Dispatch: "Major Change: Unemployment to Drop by Three"

2. Players will have five minutes to read the headlines and discuss them with each other. At the end of the five minutes, the students will write down their guesses for how the unemployment rate will change. For example, a player may write that unemployment will "increase by one."

3. The instructor will then announce how unemployment actually changed. Each student receives one point for each point by which he was incorrect. For example, if a student thought unemployment would increase by one and it actually decreased by one, he would receive 2 points; if unemployment increased by two, then he would receive only one point. *Remember, the goal is to have the fewest number of points.*

If three students made the predictions shown below, and the actual change in unemployment was an increase of two points, then the students would receive the following number of points:

	Prediction	Points
Student A	+4	2
Student B	0	2
Student C	−1	3

After the instructor announces how unemployment changed, the round is over.

The instructor begins the next round by posting a new set of headlines. The winner is the player with the fewest number of points after five rounds.

NAME:

GUESSES FOR GAME 13: MEDIA

	Prediction	Actual Unemployment	Points
Round 1 (Practice Round)			
Round 2			
Round 3			
Round 4			
Round 5			
Round 6			

Final Number of Points: _____

NAME:

REFLECTIONS ON GAME 13: MEDIA

1. How well did you do in the game? Did your guesses become better as the game progressed?

2. Which newspapers were the most helpful? Which were the most biased? How do you know?

3. How important was it to talk to other players? Why?

4. How did your understanding of the newspapers and their biases change over the course of the game?

GAME 14   Tax and Spend

One of the most basic powers of government is the power to tax. Governments as small as local school boards to those as large as the U.S. government must decide how to raise taxes and how to spend their revenue. Should the taxes be raised through a progressive income tax which taxes the income of wealthier citizens at a higher rate than other citizens? Should taxes be raised through a flat tax that taxes every citizen's income at the same rate? Or, should revenue be raised through property or sales taxes? Once the government collects the taxes, how should it spend the money? These are the basic questions asked by public policy-makers. In this game, you will sit on a committee that is deciding on a budget. What kind of budget will you create?

GOAL

The goal of this game is to win the most points.

RULES

Players will divide into groups of seven. Each player picks a slip of paper at random from a hat. The slip of paper will be labeled one of Players 1 through 7, designating which district the player is to represent. Each group of seven is a budget committee that must decide how to raise and then spend government revenue. Each committee must decide on a budget, which involves making two choices.

First, what type of tax system should the government use? There are three choices.

- The current system is a progressive income tax system that taxes wealthier citizens at a higher rate than poorer citizens. It also has many deductions and credits that give tax breaks to families and homeowners. If the group chooses this system then it will be able allocate 40 points to address policy issues.

- A flat tax system would eliminate most or all of the deductions and credits and give everyone the same tax rate. Those with higher incomes would pay the same rate as others but would pay less in actual dollars than they pay under the current system. This difference would result in a smaller budget. If the group chooses this system then it will be able allocate 35 points to address policy issues.

- A sales tax system would tax people only on what they buy. This system would result in a much smaller budget. If the group chooses this system then it will be able allocate 30 points to address policy issues.

Because each tax system benefits different types of people, each player's district will be affected differently by each plan. Each player will lose the following number of points under the three tax systems.

Number of Points Player Loses

	Current System	Flat Tax	Sales Tax
Player 1	3 points	3 points	4 points
Player 2	4 points	4 points	4 points
Player 3	5 points	4 points	4 points
Player 4	6 points	5 points	4 points
Player 5	7 points	6 points	4 points
Player 6	7 points	6 points	5 points
Player 7	9 points	8 points	5 points

For example, if the committee chooses the current system, then the budget will be 40 points and Player 1 will lose 3 points. If the group chooses the sales tax plan, then the budget will be only 30 points and Player 1 will lose 4 points.

Second, the committee must decide how many points to "spend" addressing a series of public policy issues. Each player has different first and second priority issues that he would like to see government address:

	First priority	Second priority
Player 1	Civil rights	Crime
Player 2	Crime	Education
Player 3	Education	Environment
Player 4	Environment	Healthcare
Player 5	Healthcare	Housing
Player 6	Housing	Transportation
Player 7	Transportation	Civil rights

Each player will receive points if their committee allocates points to the player's first and second priority issues:

First priority: 2 × points allocated by committee

Second priority: 1 × points allocated by committee

For example, if the government decides to give 2 points to help the environment, then Player 4 receives four points ($2 \times 2 = 4$), Player 3 receives two points ($1 \times 2 = 2$), and the rest of the players receive no additional points.

Each committee has 20 minutes to decide on a budget. A final budget must have the following items (see budget sheet):

1. The signatures of at least 4 players—a majority of the committee must agree with the budget.

2. A choice of tax system: current system (40 points), flat tax (35 points), or sales tax (30 points).

3. An allocation of the points given to each policy area. The number of points cannot be greater than the points from the tax system. Therefore, if you choose the sales tax, you cannot allocate more than 30 points.

At the end of the 20-minute time period, the instructor will announce how each committee decided to tax and to spend its revenue. The class will then discuss some of the differences.

Players are competing against all of the players in the class, not just those on their committee. The winner is the player who has the most points.

One final important rule: *If at the end of the time period your committee cannot agree on a budget, then everyone in the group receives zero points!*

SAMPLE BUDGET

Choose ONE	Number of Points in Taxes
Current system	
Flat tax	
Sales tax	30

	Number of Points Spent on Each Issue
Civil rights	2
Crime	3
Education	0
Environment	6
Healthcare	2
Housing	7
Transportation	10
Total	30

Number of Points Each Person Received

	First priority × 2	+ Second priority	− Taxes	= Total
Player 1	4	3	3	4
Player 2	6	0	4	2
Player 3	0	6	4	2
Player 4	12	2	5	9
Player 5	4	7	6	5
Player 6	14	10	6	18
Player 7	20	2	8	14

NAME:

COMMITTEE BUDGET

Choose ONE	Number of Points in Taxes
Current system	
Flat tax	
Sales tax	

Number of Points Spent on Each Issue

Civil rights	
Crime	
Education	
Environment	
Healthcare	
Housing	
Transportation	
Total	

Number of Points Each Person Received

	First priority $\times 2$	+ Second priority	– Taxes	= Total
Player 1				
Player 2				
Player 3				
Player 4				
Player 5				
Player 6				
Player 7				

Players' Signatures:

1.   2.

3.   4.

REFLECTIONS ON GAME 14: TAX AND SPEND

1. How fair was the tax system that your committee chose? Was there another system that you thought was more fair? Why?

2. How fair was the way that your committee allocated points? Would a different allocation have been more fair? Why?

3. How well did you do in this game? Looking back, how could you have done better?

4. How different were the budgets that the various committees chose? Were they very similar or very different from each other?

GAME 15 Fairness

In the United States, most people think that government policies should be just and fair. Political philosophers, however, have spent a good deal of time and ink debating the meaning of "fairness" and "justice." Is it fair to redistribute money from the rich to the poor? Is it just to give everyone the same tax rate or to have a progressive tax system?

One view of fairness or justice is that someone is being fair when he makes a decision without knowing if he will personally benefit from the decision. In this game, you will try to come up with the best "fair" budget that you can. This game has the same rules as Game 14: Tax and Spend but with an important twist—in this game, you must come up with a budget *before* you know your player number.

GOAL

The goal of this game is to win the most points.

RULES

Players will divide into groups of seven. Each group of seven is a budget committee that must decide how to raise and then spend government revenue. Each committee must decide on a budget which involves making two choices.

First, what type of tax system should the government use? There are three choices.

- The current system is a progressive income tax system that taxes wealthier citizens at a higher rate than poorer citizens. It also has many deductions and credits that give tax breaks to families and homeowners. If the group chooses this system then it will be able to allocate 40 points to address policy issues.

- A flat tax system would eliminate most or all of the deductions and credits and give everyone the same tax rate. This would mean that those with higher incomes would pay the same rate as others, but would pay less in actual dollars than they pay under the current system. This difference would result in a smaller budget. If the group chooses this system then it will be able to allocate 35 points to address policy issues.

- A sales tax system would tax people only on what they buy. This system would result in a much smaller budget. If the group chooses this system then it will be able to allocate 30 points to address policy issues.

Because each tax system benefits different types of people, each player's district will be affected differently by each plan. Each player will lose the following number of points under the three tax systems.

Number of Points Player Loses

	Current System	Flat Tax	Sales Tax
Player 1	3 points	3 points	4 points
Player 2	4 points	4 points	4 points
Player 3	5 points	4 points	4 points
Player 4	6 points	5 points	4 points
Player 5	7 points	6 points	4 points
Player 6	7 points	6 points	5 points
Player 7	9 points	8 points	5 points

For example, if the committee chooses the current system, then the budget will be 40 points and Player 1 will lose 3 points. If the group chooses the sales tax plan, then the budget will be only 30 points and Player 1 will lose 4 points.

Second, the committee must decide how many points to "spend" addressing a series of public policy issues. Each player has first and second priority issues that he would like to see government address:

	First priority	Second priority
Player 1	Civil rights	Crime
Player 2	Crime	Education
Player 3	Education	Environment
Player 4	Environment	Healthcare
Player 5	Healthcare	Housing
Player 6	Housing	Transportation
Player 7	Transportation	Civil rights

Each player will receive points if their committee allocates points to the player's first and second priority issues:

First priority: $2 \times$ points allocated to address issue

Second priority: $1 \times$ points allocated to address issue

For example, if the government decides to give 2 points to help the environment, then Player 4 receives four points ($2 \times 2 = 4$), Player 3 receives two points ($1 \times 2 = 2$), and the rest of the players receive no additional points.

Each committee has 20 minutes to decide on a budget. A final budget must have the following items (see budget sheet):

1. The signatures of at least 4 players—a majority of the committee must agree with the budget.

2. A choice of tax system: current system (40 points), flat tax (35 points), and sales tax (30 points).

3. An allocation of the points given to each policy area. The number of points cannot be greater than the points from the tax system. Therefore, if you choose the sales tax, you cannot allocate more than 30 points.

After the committee agrees on a budget, each player draws a number at random from a hat, designating Player 1, Player 2, etc.

At the end of the 20-minute time period, the instructor will announce how each committee decided to tax and spend its revenue. The class will then discuss some of the differences.

Players are competing against all of the players in the class, not just those on their committee. The winner is the player (or players) who has the most points.

One final important rule: *If at the end of the time period your committee cannot agree on a budget, then everyone in the group receives zero points!*

SAMPLE BUDGET

Choose ONE	Number of Points in Taxes
Current system	
Flat tax	
Sales tax	30

	Number of Points Spent on Each Issue
Civil rights	2
Crime	3
Education	0
Environment	6
Healthcare	2
Housing	7
Transportation	10
Total	30

Number of Points Each Person Received

	First priority × 2	+ Second priority	− Taxes	= Total
Player 1	4	3	3	4
Player 2	6	0	4	2
Player 3	0	6	4	2
Player 4	12	2	5	9
Player 5	4	7	6	5
Player 6	14	10	6	18
Player 7	20	2	8	14

COMMITTEE BUDGET

Choose ONE	Number of Points in Taxes
Current system	
Flat tax	
Sales tax	

Number of Points Spent on Each Issue

Civil rights	
Crime	
Education	
Environment	
Healthcare	
Housing	
Transportation	
Total	

Number of Points Each Person Received

	First priority × 2	+ Second priority	– Taxes	= Total
Player 1				
Player 2				
Player 3				
Player 4				
Player 5				
Player 6				
Player 7				

Players' Signatures: 1. 2.

3. 4.

REFLECTIONS ON GAME 15: FAIRNESS

1. How fair was the tax system that your committee chose? Was it more fair than the one chosen in the Tax and Spend game? Why?

2. How fair was the way that your committee allocated points? Was it more fair than the allocation chosen in the Tax and Spend game? Why?

3. Did you do better than you did in the Tax and Spend game? Why or why not?

4. How different were the budgets that the committees chose? Were they either very similar or very different from each other?

GAME 16   Foreign Policy

Creating good public policy is always difficult. It is even more difficult with foreign policy because nations must try to change the actions of other sovereign nations. The United States, for example, cannot simply mandate changes in another nation's policies. Instead, the United States must rely on diplomacy, bargaining, and at times military force. While international organizations such as the United Nations, World Health Organization, and North Atlantic Treaty Organization help shape policies, there is no world government that can legitimately usurp the powers of sovereign nations. As a result, nations interact much like in a state of nature. In this game, we return to Game 1: State of Nature. However, here we add an important feature of the global system—the economic, political, and historical ties between nations.

As in the original State of Nature game, there is inequality. There are seven nations and each nation has an assigned amount of "power."

Nation	Power
Nation 1	10
Nation 2	40
Nation 3	70
Nation 4	60
Nation 5	30
Nation 6	50
Nation 7	20

Also, no international law is enforced. You can make treaties and agreements, but there is no government to enforce these treaties.

There are *two* important differences between the original State of Nature game and this one on foreign policy.

First, in this game you get points if your allies survive each round. Points are awarded based on the following table.

Number of Points Received
If the Following Other Nations Survive the Round

	Nation 1	Nation 2	Nation 3	Nation 4	Nation 5	Nation 6	Nation 7
Nation 1	—	20	20	40	10	10	10
Nation 2	20	—	20	40	10	10	10
Nation 3	20	20	—	40	10	10	10
Nation 4	20	20	40	—	20	30	30
Nation 5	30	30	30	20	—	50	30
Nation 6	10	10	10	10	40	—	10
Nation 7	10	10	10	10	40	40	—

For example, Nation 1 receives 20 points if Nation 2 survives, 20 points if Nation 3 survives, 40 points if Nation 4 survives, etc.

Second, in this game slavery is not an option. You cannot survive by giving all of your property to another nation. You must work out a way to survive on your own.

GOAL

The goal of each nation is to survive and have the most "power." The winner will be the nation that survives the game with the most points.

RULES

At the beginning of each round, nations will be asked (in order from the nation with the least points to the nation with the most points at the start of the round) what they want to do. Each nation has four choices:

1. Invest all points and receive a 10% return.

2. Give some points to another nation as part of a treaty. Remember, treaties are only as good at the reputation of the nations that agree to them.

3. Attack a nation with less property and take up to 20 points from that nation. *If the nation being attacked is left with no points, then it is eliminated from the game.*

At the *end of each round*, each nation that survives will be given extra points based on how well its allies did. After these points are given out, a new round will begin.

SCORECARD FOR GAME 16: FOREIGN POLICY

To help keep track of how the game is going, record the decision of each nation
and how many points each nation has at the end of the round.

	Round 1		Round 2		Round 3	
	Decision	**Final Points**	**Decision**	**Final Points**	**Decision**	**Final Points**
Nation 1						
Nation 2						
Nation 3						
Nation 4						
Nation 5						
Nation 6						
Nation 7						

REFLECTIONS ON GAME 16: FOREIGN POLICY

1. Looking back on how you did in the first State of Nature game, did you perform better or worse this time? Why was the outcome different?

2. How important were trade alliances and allies in this game?

3. How well do you think this game mirrors what actually happens in international politics? What features are accurate? Which ones are inaccurate?

4. Some people think that if we increase trade with other countries, there would be more peace in the world. Do you think that this is true? What do you think could be done to help increase peace?

5. Did any of the nations remind you of actual countries? In what ways were they like these countries? Were any similar to the United States?